1ˢᵗ Edition

BUILT TO LAST: The keys to Longevity.

By

Steve McCain. MD

Copyright @ 2023 Steve McCain. MD

All rights reserved

TABLE OF CONTENTS

Dedication

This book is dedicated to God almighty, all my clients that I have been able to enlighten on how to keep fit and live healthy lives. I also dedicate it to my beautiful wife who has always been very supportive and lastly my two beautiful daughters who want to follow in their fathers

footsteps.

Introduction

A healthy lifestyle is necessary

for us to live long and happy

lives, this is something we must

commit to, it involves getting

rid of unhealthy habits and

embracing the healthy, the

most important fact is that a lot

of the factors that will enable us

live long and healthy lives are

within our control, hence it

depends on us to either commit

and live long and healthy lives

or not, the ball is in your court.

Why you need this book

This book *"BUILT TO LAST:*

The keys to Longevity." was

published from the experience of so

many clients who had issues with

living healthy, happy lives, which

was mostly due to ignorance, there

are little things we ignore, feeling

they are not important and because

we don't see the consequences

immediately, we assume they don't have any impact on us but most of the time, this things keep piling up in our bodies and we don't notice their effect until we are much older.

In Ten concise chapters, the author has discussed several issues that destroy our health and shortens the lifespan of so many of us, he also discussed possible solutions to

ensure that we live long and

healthy lives.

Dr Steve McCain is a health expert who has enlightened so many people on what to avoid and what to embrace in order to live long and healthy lives and due to the commitment of so many of them who got rid of the unhealthy habits, they have been able to live healthy lives and even saved a lot of money as a result of cutting down on unhealthy products they once purchased. Get this book right now and enlighten yourself on how to live a

healthy life.

Chapter One

Avoid Ultra-Processed food

Avoid eating foods that has undergone a lot of processing to change them from their original state. They have the most additives, are frequently colored, shaped, or sweetened artificially, and it's often hard to tell what's in them.

These includes but isn't restricted to wafers, cereals, chicken tenders, sweets, chips, ramen noodles, sausages, pizza, frozen suppers among others.

Why should you stay away from foods that have been Ultra processed?

 Foods that have been extremely processed typically lack vitamins, minerals, and fiber, but thcy also havc a lot of calories. They also have more added sugar, sodium, unhealthy fats, and additives, all of which have been linked to a higher risk of developing chronic diseases.

Ultra-processed foods have been found to alter the body's satiety process and glycemic response, affecting metabolism and cardiovascular function. Additionally, the onset and progression of cardio-metabolic disorders are sparked in large part by a number of substances produced during food processing.

Most foods that have been extremely processed have a lot of sugar added to them. These empty calories can cause long-term illness.

They have flavors that people like, like sweet, salty, and fatty, which can make people eat more than they should. We sometimes eat until we feel sick because our brains prevent us from feeling full in favor of providing us with a satisfying experience from eating processed foods.

Foods that have been extremely processed are less filling and have a higher blood sugar level than foods that have been minimally processed. They generally have more calories and sugar, are lower in protein and fiber, and are linked to obesity. Eating them replaces healthier, nutrient-rich foods that you could be eating instead, like crisp vegetables rather than pop and chips. Many of them are snacks that encourage mindless eating and eliminate the need or desire for real food. In addition, they contain unhealthy fats like corn oil and ingredients that promote inflammation, such as refined sugars (carbohydrates).

Foods that have been extremely processed are addictive. Some parts of the brain are affected by sugar and highly gratifying junk food as cocaine.

When compared to whole, unprocessed foods, which are organic when eaten, processed foods lack essential nutrients. Even overweight people can become malnourished, necessitating nutrient-dense diets.

When we digest processed foods, we burn fewer calories. Genuine food varieties contain more fiber, which requires more energy use to separate it.

The following is a list of ultra-processed foods and their harmful effects on our health:

- ➢ Chips: Chips' sodium content may be harmful to your cardiovascular health. A high sodium intake can raise blood pressure, which can cause heart disease, stroke, heart failure, and kidney disease.

- ➢ Dark Chocolate: Chocolate also has a lot of sugar and saturated fat. It has a lot of energy and calories, and eating too much of it can make you gain weight, which can increase your risk of heart disease.

➢ Candy: Overindulging in candy can increase chronic inflammation and raise blood pressure, both of which are pathological pathways to heart disease.

➢ Sweetened Cereals: Sweetened cereals can make you gain weight and even contribute to chronic diseases like diabetes and heart disease over time.

➢ Packaged Soups: Even though canned soups often contain lentils, carrots, and celery, they often contain a lot of sodium, which can cause heart disease. People that are

already battling with heart disease might

want to keep an eye on how much sodium is

in their soup.

➢ Chicken Nuggets: Depending on how they

are made, chicken nuggets have a lot of bad

ingredients like oil, sugar, and bleached

wheat. They also have a lot of fat and

sodium. Those ingredients may enhance the

flavor of the meaty morsels, but they are not

as beneficial to your overall health,

particularly if you consume them frequently

in large quantities.

> Hot Dog: Hot dogs are a type of processed meat, which belongs to the group of foods that are known as carcinogens. Processed meats especially contain saturated fat, which clogs the arteries and has been linked to heart diseases.

> Fries: Fats are digested by the body more slowly than carbohydrates and proteins, and because they contain more calories because of how they are cooked, fries will stay in your stomach for much longer than healthier food would.

Chapter Two

Reduce Stress

Life expectancy is influenced by a person's quality of life as well as traditional lifestyle-related risk factors, such as excessive stress.

Stress is a normal part of life, but it can shorten your life if you become accustomed to stressing over the smallest details. You should learn how to de-stress in order to prolong your life and improve your health and quality of life.

The following are some negative effects of stress:

> Heart Diseases: The sympathetic nervous system, which is the automatic part of the

nervous system that affects many organs, including the heart, can be activated by stress, which can have a negative effect on the heart's activity. The proper functioning of the heart is altered in a number of ways by stressful situations like these. In addition to increasing the heart rate and pumping action, sudden stress also causes the arteries to constrict, limiting blood flow, increases the likelihood of a blood clot clogging an artery.

➢ Improper functioning of the digestive system: Numerous hormones serve as mediators between the brain and intestine, which are interwoven. Therefore, it should not come as a surprise that prolonged stress can disrupt the digestive system, irritating the large intestine and resulting in cramping, bloating, diarrhea, and constipation. Excessive creation of acids in the stomach   may likewise create an excruciating stomach upset.

> Diabetes: Insulin resistance, a condition in which the body is unable to effectively use insulin to regulate glucose levels, has been linked to chronic stress. Diabetes is primarily caused by insulin resistance.

➤ Migraines: Headaches are one of the most common physical ailments caused by stress. The muscle-tension headache is the most prevalent type of headache, typically brought on by muscle contractions in the shoulders, neck, forehead, and scalp.

➤ High blood pressure: A high blood pressure is called hypertension. Our blood pressure rises when we are under a great deal of stress.

➤ Asthma: The main windpipe doesn't work well in asthma, a respiratory condition that makes it hard to breathe. An allergic reaction, stress, emotional responses like

rage, or even laughing too loudly can all

trigger asthma attacks.

Chapter Three

Quit Smoking

Smoking can prompt continuous entanglements and long haul consequences for your body framework. Even though smoking can make you more likely to get certain diseases over time, like cancer, glaucoma, and problems with blood clotting, some of the effects on your body happen right away.

There is no safe method of smoking. You won't be able to avoid the health risks by switching to a cigar, pipe, e-cigarette instead of smoking.

Smoking has numerous negative effects on our health and well-being; some of these include lung damage, Smoking can damage your airways and the small air sacs (alveoli) in your lungs, which can lead to lung disease.

The cells in your lungs and airways that make mucus expand and multiply when you smoke. The amount of mucus increases and thickens as a result.

This excessive mucus cannot be effectively eliminated by your lungs. As a result, when you cough the mucus remains in your airways and blocks them. Infections can also spread through this extra mucus.

Smoking makes your lungs age more quickly and makes it harder for your body's natural defenses to keep you safe from infection.

Lungs are irritated and inflamed. Indeed, even a couple of cigarettes cause bothering and hacking.

Additionally, smoking can harm your lungs and lung tissue. This diminishes the quantity of air spaces and veins in the lungs, bringing about less oxygen to the other parts of your body.

> Loss of skin elasticity: Your skin's loss of supply of collagen is one of the main effects of smoking on the skin. The protein that gives your skin its elasticity is called collagen. Smoking increases the production of an enzyme that degrades collagen, thereby reducing elasticity and giving your

skin an aged, sagging and wrinkled appearance.

Smokers have distinctive skin wrinkle patterns, around the eyes and lines around the mouth. The mouth-lines are thought to be caused by sucking on a cigarette, which builds up over time and has added the collagen-depleting effects of smoking. The increased squinting that occurs when smoke is directed toward the eyes is thought to be the cause of the wrinkles around the eyes.

> Gum Disease: Smoking can stain teeth, cause gum disease, cause tooth loss, and, in the worst-case scenario, cause mouth cancer. The nicotine and tar in tobacco cause teeth

stains, which is one of the effects of smoking. It can make your teeth yellow in an exceptionally brief time frame, and weighty smokers frequently grumble that their teeth are practically brown after smoking for a long time.

Smokers are more likely to develop gum disease through the production of bacterial plaque. Because smoking reduces the amount of oxygen in the bloodstream, the infected gums cannot heal. Smoking increases the amount of dental plaque and accelerates the progression of gum disease compared to nonsmokers. Adult tooth loss is still primarily caused by gum disease.

> Poor Vision: Smoking has the same negative
effects on your body as it does on your eyes.
If you smoke, you run the risk of developing
serious vision issues that could result in
blindness or vision loss.

Nicotine and carbon monoxide accelerate atherosclerosis and interfere with lipid homeostasis, resulting in fatty deposits in the blood vessels, it increases platelet aggregation, and it can induce blood clotting. Additionally, various components of cigarette smoke can lead to an acute constriction of the ciliary arteries, which reduces blood flow to the eye. Tobacco smoke contains free radicals that reduce the presence of protective antioxidants and, as a result, can cause oxidative damage to the retina. Heavy metals such as cadmium, lead, and copper that are found in tobacco smoke can accumulate in the lens and cause cataracts.

> ➤ Weakened Immune System: Smoking can impair the body's ability to fight diseases, it can also destroy the immune system. The body's defense against disease and infection is the immune system. It works to combat everything from serious illnesses like cancer to cold and flu viruses.

Since smoking can debilitate the human body, it's nothing unexpected that the individuals who smoke are more helpless against Coronavirus. This could be because some smokers already have a smaller lung capacity, making them more likely to get COVID-19 and have severe symptoms that need to be treated in a hospital. In contrast, smokers who already have a condition like lung disease also have a much higher risk of contracting COVID-19 because their immune systems are already weak.

It is evident that smoking can have a significant impact on the functioning of your immune system, which plays a crucial role in preventing illness. Your immune system will have a better chance of protecting you as it should if it is no longer exposed to the nicotine, tar, and harmful chemicals in cigarettes. Not only will quitting smoking improve your immune system, but it will also

improve your overall health.

Chapter Four

Don't hold grudges.

When you hold a grudge, you keep feeling resentment, anger, or other negative emotions long after someone has hurt you. Typically, it is in response to something that has already taken place; other times, a resentment may arise simply from the perception that someone is against you or intends to harm you—regardless of whether or not they actually do so. Grudges frequently include persistent angry or bitter thoughts about the person or event that caused your ill will.

Basically, it's bad for you to hold a grudge. It entraps you out of resentment and makes you inclined to constant rumination as opposed to moving on with your life. Although you may believe that harboring animosity is harmful to the person you are angry with, in the end, it is only you who suffers as a result.

A grudge does not solve your problem and is highly unlikely to make you feel any better. It also keeps you stuck in the past—trapped in an unpleasant event or interaction that causes you distress—and prevents you from coping with or resolving the issue. Research shows that focusing on negative emotions rather than resolving them is also harmful—and can even make for an unpleasant demeanor and significantly erode your well-being. Holding on to grudges can increase your stress levels, which can then contribute to

high blood pressure, heart problems, lowered

immunity, and inflammation.

Chapter Five

Embrace Positive relationships

Positive relationships are important because being alone can have major negative effects on your health. Depression can prompt disturbed rest, increased circulatory strain, and sometimes cause suicidal thoughts. It can have an effect on your immune system and lower your level of overall contentment. Depression, suicidal ideation, and antisocial behavior are all linked to loneliness.

Older people are especially at risk. The human body and psyche are massively mind boggling things. They benefit from interaction with other people in a variety of ways, depending on the specific stimulus. For instance, the sound propensities for the others around you can subliminally impact your own. Good relationships can help you manage the stress that we all experience, in addition to preventing stress. Additionally, scientists have proposed that "caring behaviors trigger the release of hormones that reduce stress." This means that you and the person you care about will feel less stressed when you care for them as much as you do. Give what you get! Being in good relationships makes you happy, and people who are happy live longer and are healthier. Wellbeing and joy are more than unmistakable elements in the person. They become intertwined and interact, influencing one another. Healthy people are happier people, and happy people are healthier. Positive relationships with the people who matter most to us are what make us most happy.

There are various ways of meeting wonderful people. Just keep in mind to ensure your safety whenever you meet new people. Meeting in a public place, for example, can be a good strategy where other people are present.

Joining a sports team, joining a hiking or hobby group, or volunteering are other options. Call your neighborhood board to learn about nearby gatherings or projects, or visit your nearby public venue or library - there's continuously something occurring locally.

Try a few different strategies to see which ones work best for you because not all strategies are suitable for everyone. Try something else if the first thing you try doesn't work.

Sharing your time, experiences, and stories with other people and listening to them is part of the concept of social connection. You will gradually develop a group of people in your life who care about you as well as about you. Both your psyche and body will enjoy the benefits.

Chapter Six

Avoid fear and worry

A lot of factors lead us to fear and worry. Not having sufficient cash, losing your employment, disappointment or dismissal, sickness or agony… And, surprisingly, the apprehension about death, which is a definitive trepidation for some individuals. The majority of our apprehensions are held under control by our capacity to manage our considerations and by changing our circumstances or viewpoint. Be that as it may, when we don't or can't make those changes, our apprehensions can become overpowering and hazardous.

We dread a wide range of things, both genuine and

unrealistic. We long for significance, purpose,

love, acceptance, association, closeness, delight,

security, opportunity, and achievement. It's

actually our needs and endeavors to satisfy and

keep up with our necessities that are the reason for

all our worry, stress, and tension. It's no big

surprise all of us are so worried!

Stress is feeling uncomfortable or being

excessively worried about a circumstance or issue.

With extreme stressing, your psyche and body go

into overdrive as you continually center around

"what could happen?"

Amidst exorbitant stressing, you might go through

a lot of anxiety, even frenzy during waking hours.

Constant stressing can influence your day to day routine so much that it might disrupt your hunger, way of life, connections, rest, and occupation. Many individuals who stress exorbitantly are so tension ridden that they look for alleviation in destructive way of life, for example, cigarette smoking, binge drinking and drugs.

Fear is a significant and sadly extremely normal disruptor of regular daily existence. Notwithstanding, steady sensations of stress can make it challenging to relate with individuals around you and any action you participate in. In the event that you experience the ill effects of persistent nervousness, you most likely have an extremely difficult time zeroing in on anything more beside the distress you feel. Unfortunately, persistent tension accomplishes more than influence your life quality. It can likewise altogether abbreviate your life expectancy.

Many individuals who experience the ill effects of persistent fear use medications or liquor to advance liberating sensation. Thus, their futures and their life expectancy decline significantly additionally given that these people likewise experience the ill effects of the unexpected impacts of substance misuse. Fear can make changes the pulse and blood dissemination. Tension portrays a lot of issues that cause stress, anxiety, and dread. These sensations of fear obstruct day to day existence.

Chapter Seven

Sleep Properly

Always ensure that you have your full night rest.

Not getting sufficient rest depletes your psychological capacities and seriously endangers your wellbeing. Science has connected insufficient sleep with various medical issues, from weight gain to a debilitated safe framework.

Getting under 7 hours of rest consistently can negatively influence your whole body. Your body needs rest, similarly as it needs air and food to work at its ideal. During rest, your body mends itself and reestablishes its substance balance. Your mind fashions groundbreaking insight associations and ensures proper memory functioning.

Without enough rest, your body and mind won't work properly. You may likewise find it hard to think or learn new things. Lack of sleep additionally adversely influences your psychological capacities. You might feel more eager or inclined to mood swings. Assuming lack of sleep continues for a long time, you could begin to see or hear things that aren't actually there. Lack of rest can likewise set off madness in individuals who have bipolar temperament problem.

While you rest, your body produces antibodies and cytokines. It utilizes these substances to fight harmful microorganisms and infections.

Lack of sleep keeps your system from functioning properly. In the event that you don't get sufficient rest, your body will most likely be unable to fight off sickness, and it might likewise take you longer to recuperate from ailment. Lack of sleep can likewise aggravate existing respiratory sicknesses, like constant lung diseases.

Apart from eating excessively and not working out, lack of sleep is another main factor for becoming overweight and hefty.

Insufficient sleep can likewise cause you to feel too drained to even consider working out. Lack of sleep likewise makes your body produce less insulin after you eat. Insulin assists with reducing your glucose (glucose) level.

These disturbances can prompt diabetes mellitus
and heftiness.

The pituitary organ discharges development
chemical over the course of every day, except
sufficient rest and exercise likewise help the
arrival of this chemical.

The most essential treatment for insufficient sleep
is getting a satisfactory measure of rest, commonly
7 to 8 hours.

Chapter Eight

Exercise Regularly

We all realize that exercise can assist you with keeping fit, decrease weight, further develop equilibrium and lower your chances of some illnesses, like coronary illness. Exercise helps reduces the risk of issues with the cardiovascular system, disease, and diabetes, the advantages of regular exercise are uncountable, as endless studies have shown. Some of the advantages of regular exercise are discussed below:

> ➤ It brightens your mood: Regular exercise has a way of making you youthful regardless

of your age. Those that exercise regularly
always look younger than those who don't.

➢ It builds your energy: Exercise helps you
build lean muscle, teaches you discipline
and perseverance, it ensures that oxygen
courses throughout your body, and keeps
your cardiovascular framework in excellent
condition. You'll feel more stimulated to
handle your daily activities, it also reduces
the risk of coronary diseases.

➢ It ensures that you sleep better: Those that
exercise regularly sleep a lot better than
those that don't. Not getting sufficient rest is

one more component connected to sudden breakdown, so getting the required 7 to 8 hours every night is necessary.

➢ It helps fight some infections: Regular exercise reduces the risk of certain illnesses and untimely death.

➢ It aids digestion: Exercise helps the body absorb of nutrients into the blood stream a lot more easily.

Chapter Nine

Avoid Alcohol

Alcohol can be likened to poison that in excess can cause a lot of harm to the body. The consequences of excess alcohol intake are diseases that can fundamentally shortens a human life.

A lot of fatal accidents are as a result of driving under the influence of alcohol. By and large, 33% of fatal accidents are as a result of excessive alcohol intake. Long term liquor misuse can likewise diminish ones future because of a debilitated system. Excess consumption of alcohol can make it harder for the body to fight infections.

For instance, those that drink excessively are at a greater risk of contracting lung diseases like pneumonia and tuberculosis than individuals who don't drink at all.

> Excessive alcohol intake increases the chances of heart-related diseases. For instance, the more you drink, the more probable you are to have hypertension.

> The liver processes liquor as acetaldehyde, which is a poisonous compound. Alcohol excites the liver and furthermore obstructs its capacity to use fats. This makes fat gather around the liver. Excessive alcohol intake may cause liver cirrhosis or hepatitis. Liver

Cirrhosis occurs when alcohol so completely scars the liver that the liver fails. When the liver stops separating blood, the other organs of the body start to malfunction. This is a dangerous condition which kills a lot of people. Cirrhosis grows slowly, maybe much throughout the span of quite a few years, and once in a while individuals don't know that they have cirrhosis until it is too late.

Chapter Ten

Benefits of healthy living

> ➢ It improves your physical health: Eating
> fresh and nutritious food has a positive
> effect on your wellbeing in general. It
> reduces the risk of chronic diseases such as
> diabetes, coronary illness, hypertension,
> stroke among others. It prevents unnecessary
> weight gain.

> ➢ Improves your psychological well-being:

A healthy way of life prevents or reduces mental

breakdown and keeps you in a sound state of mind.

Exercise improves your psychological health by

reducing uneasiness, stress, sorrow and negative state of mind, and by working on mental capability. Muscle-reinforcing exercises ought to be remembered for a work-out daily schedule, two times per week. This should include opposition band practices and bodyweight activities like pushups, thrusts and squats. High-impact works out, like strolling, cultivating, swimming, running and cycling, have been known to decrease nervousness and misery.

One to two hours of activity each week have been known to reduce the chances of feeling depressed.

> ➢ It saves you a lot of money: Quitting undesirable activities like smoking, drinking sweet soda pops, or drinking liquor in excess

can save you a lot of cash since you will not need to buy them any longer.

If you cook at home instead of requesting take-out, you'll have the opportunity of preparing fresh organic home-made meals such as fresh vegetables from the farmers market which have not undergone any significant processing and does not have all the preservatives that tend to increase the shelf life of most of those products.

You will find out that these fresh veggies are a lot more economical and better for your health than all the ultra-processed meals.

When you live a healthy lifestyle you will fall sick less often and will not have to go to the hospital as often and save a lot of money you would have spent on being admitted at the hospital, buying

medications. Think of the cost of a big pack of

chips and compare with purchasing bananas at the

market. Then consider the different effect they

both have on your health.

Going to the doctor is not something terrible. It's a

good idea to go for regular check-ups to be sure

that you are in a good state of health. Furthermore,

on occasion, you could feel the need to make an

impromptu visit, whether you notice something

else with your body or you feel ill.

However, unhealthy living can increase the

number of visits to the doctor.

> It improves your mood: When you work out,

   your body releases endorphins, which can

improve your mental health and happiness.

It might appear glaringly evident that this

would add to better psychological well-

being and joy.